THE 14-MINUTE MARCEL PROUST

The 14-Minute Marcel Proust

A Very Short Guide to the Greatest Novel Ever Written

Stephen Fall

Fallbook Press 2010

Introduction

How the project began

I set out to read *Swann's Way* more than once before a pal challenged me to read the whole of Proust's gargantuan novel with him. Every Wednesday, on his way to the law office where he worked as a low-level attorney, he'd stop by my room (it had a kitchen but wasn't really an apartment). We'd drink coffee, smoke, and talk about what we'd read during the week. Egging each other on in this fashion, we finished the book before the year was out.

Ten years later, I read the novel again—and aloud—to my wife over the course of two winters. (One of the French deconstructionists, arguing that one can't just study a novel by itself, because it's a collaborative venture between the author and the reader, tried to cinch his case by pointing out: "After all, who has read every word of *À la recherche du temps perdu?*" It pleased me hugely to be able to say, if only silently, "I did!")

That was the handsome two-volume Random House edition of the novel, entitled *Remembrance of Things Past*, the first six books rendered into English by Charles Scott Moncrieff and the seventh by Frederick Blossom. (Scott Moncrieff died before finishing his task, which is probably the reason why Penguin decided to employ seven different translators for its 21st Century Proust.) When Terence Kilmartin's reworking came out in the 1980s, I acquired that, too, but only read pieces of it—notably book seven, *The Past Recaptured*, greatly improved over the rather lame Fred Blossom translation. Otherwise, *Remembrance of Things Past* was still hobbled by the post-Victorian prose of Scott Moncrieff, or so it seemed to me.

Then came the new Penguin editions, the first four volumes of which have now been published in the United States by Viking. After reading a rave review of volume two—*In the Shadow of Young Girls in Flower*—I realized that I would have to read it. On second thought, I

1

decided to start from the beginning with the new *Swann's Way*. It was a good decision. Lydia Davis did a wonderful job with the first volume, and by the time I'd lulled Little Marcel to sleep (on page 43 in her translation), I knew that I was once again in for the long haul. So I set out to acquire a complete set of hardcover books—not so easy, as matters turned out! I read them in sequence, and I blogged about them on the internet as I read. This little book came out of that project.

But why bother?

The French have been known to boast that they have a Shakespeare for every generation, or at least for every century, while we Anglophones are stuck with Will's originals. Well, now we can say the same about Proust! Here is a Marcel for the age of the internet.

Beyond that, I've heard it argued that literary French has changed little over the past hundred years, while English most certainly has, under the battering of such writers as James Joyce and Ernest Hemingway. (Whatever you say about Charles Scott Moncrieff, he probably never read *Ulysses*, and he certainly was unfamiliar with the noisy young journalist who stormed into Paris in 1921.) However that may be, it's nice to have a freshened version of Proust's prose, and one that arguably is closer to the original than the one rendered by Scott Moncrieff in the 1920s.

Proust, Joyce, and Hemingway! It's pleasant to think that my three favorite writers once breathed the same air in Paris. Indeed, Joyce and Proust once met at a party . . . and had little or nothing to say to one another. — *Stephen Fall, September 2010*

MARCEL PROUST

A NEW TRANSLATION BY LYDIA DAVIS

Swann's Way

1 – *Swann's Way*

In French: *Du côté de chez Swann*
Also translated as: *The Way by Swann's*

The two-minute *Swann*

First we lull Little Marcel to sleep, then we join him on long walks out from Combray. One direction takes him "the Guermantes way," prefiguring the rich, beautiful, addled, and perverted clan that will people the novel to come. The other direction is 'Swann's way." On one of the latter walks, Marcel spies a girl with red hair and promptly falls in love with her, as he is prone to do. (For folks who seek symbols in literature, Swann's way is also the life of the mind, as opposed to the high society of the Guermantes.)

But the big news of this volume is the earlier love of Charles Swann for the courtesan Odette de Crecy. This section is best summarized in Swann's closing words: "To think that I wasted years of my life, that I wanted to die, that I felt my deepest love, for a woman who did not appeal to me, who was not my type!" (But note that Swann's renunciation doesn't stop him from marrying her! This he evidently does in order that their daughter may be introduced to the Duchesse de Guermantes, a sweet but rather loopy motive.)

Flash forward to Paris, where Marcel (my guess is that he is now fourteen) meets the red-haired Gilberte Swann in the Jardin des Champs Élysées and realizes his love, after a fashion.

The new Penguin/Viking edition

The American fiction writer Lydia Davis has done a masterful job at brushing up Scott Moncrieff's somewhat musty, post-Victorian prose. (Unfortunately, I can't compare her version with Proust's *Du côté de chez Swann*, for the very good reason that I've never studied French. I can suss it out, and I can buy a meal or a railway ticket, but no more.) The two versions really aren't that much different: I've compared sentences here and there, and generally only one word has been changed. But often that word is important. Scott Moncrieff, for example, will have Swann *exclaiming* something, while Davis has him *saying* it—and from what I can tell, that's what Proust was writing also. Then too, she strips out many of the intensifiers, so that Swann is now *content* with something, instead of being *quite content*. This too seems closer to the original. Finally, she often opts for the less elegant word, writing *delicious* instead of *exquisite*.

The new translations are also technically more accurate than the earlier versions, because they incorporate the latest French scholarship on Proust. I found a few typographical errors in the American edition of the new *Swann's Way*; I don't know whether they spring from the Penguin edition or were created in the course of rendering the British language into American. Except for one case (where *O* appears instead of *An*), they won't cause any confusion. (I had to go back to the French to clear that one up.)

In Britain, this first volume is titled *The Way By Swann's*, and there are a few differences in the text as well. French literary quotations remain in French; conversation is shown by dashes instead of quotation marks, and the spelling presumably is British standard.

The translator

Lydia Davis is the author of short stories, including the wonderfully titled *Samuel Johnson Is Indignant*, and one novel, *The End of the Story*. Professor of creative writing at the University of Albany, she won a $500,000 MacArthur Foundation "genius award" in 2003. She is a Chevalier of the Order of Arts and Letters.

MARCEL
PROUST

In the
Shadow of Young
Girls in Flower

A NEW TRANSLATION BY
JAMES GRIEVE

2 – *In the Shadow of Young Girls in Flower*

In French: *À l'ombre des jeunes filles en fleurs*
Also translated as: *Within a Budding Grove*

The two-minute *Young Girls*

Marcel makes quick work of Gilberte Swann. As with Swann before him, the more he loves the girl, the less interest she has in him. So he decides to put his love on ice, while maintaining his friendship with her parents.

Then, two years later, it's off to Balbec. (By my calculus, Marcel is now sixteen, but still astonishingly dependent on his mother and grandmother.) He spends a seemingly endless summer at a grand hotel on the Normandy coast, watching strange places and people become familiar to him. He becomes an improbably close friend of the Guermantes aristocrat, Robert de Saint-Loup, and of the painter Elstir (whom we met as a foolish young man belonging to Madame Verdurin's "little clan" in *Swann's Way*). He also meets the Baron de Charlus, who deigns to make a move on him, an overture which only mystifies Marcel.

More important than any of these is his acquaintance with the "little gang" of girls whom he describes as adolescent, and who sometimes behave that way, but who surely are older. (Two seem to be sitting for the *bac* or high-school leaving exam, which Proust himself passed—in economics and mathematics—just as he turned eighteen.) Marcel focuses his adoration, first on one, then on another of these young women, but it is obvious to everyone except him that Albertine Simonet will be the love of his life.

This new Penguin/Viking edition

In the second volume of his masterwork, Proust deals with the theme of friendship (including the curious sort of friendship that is carnal love). How do we bridge the gap between the stranger and the dear person he or she becomes, as friend or lover? First up: Gilberte Swann, whom Marcel first adores and then, after some pain, learns to ignore. Then there's Robert de Saint-Loup, so marvelous that the modern reader wants to kick him in the pants. And of course there is Albertine, the obsession toward which Marcel has been working all this time.

There are others, too, notably the odious and social climbing young man named Bloch. He seems to have no first name; nor does he have much in the way of physical characteristics. Bloch seems to be a year or two older than Marcel, though they were schoolmates at some point.

James Grieve swings a bit wilder than Lydia Davis in *Swann's Way*. Where Scott Moncrieff translated *petite bande* (of girls) with "little band," Grieve uses "little gang," which to an American ear sounds a bit tough. Then there is the astonishing conversation between Bloch and Marcel, referring back to the occasion when Marcel was walking in the Bois-de-Boulogne with Gilberte and her mother. Along comes Bloch, who takes his hat off to Odette without eliciting any recognition from her in turn; then, afterward, she refers to him by a name not his own.

Now, at Balbec, Bloch wants to discover *her* name, but Marcel is so puzzled by the whole affair that he doesn't oblige. Bloch then rattles on to claim an anonymous sexual romp with Madame Swann. This is how it appears in the original: *"En tous cas, tous mes compliments, me dit-il, tu n'as pas dû t'embêter avec elle. Je l'avais rencontrée quelques jours auparavant dans le train de Ceinture. Elle voulut bien dénouer la sienne en faveur de ton serviteur, je n'ai jamais passé de si bons moments et nous allions prendre toutes dispositions pour nous revoir quand une personne qu'elle connaissait eut le mauvais goût de monter à l'avant-dernière station."*

8

In *Within a Budding Grove*, Scott Moncrieff translates this quotation in words superficially close to the original, though perhaps not entirely comprehensible to the 21st Century American, who has probably never heard of a Zone railroad, never mind seen "zone" as a synonym for a woman's girdle: "Whoever she is," he went on, "hearty congratulations; you can't have been bored with her. I picked her up a few days before that on the Zone railway, where, speaking of zones, she was so kind as to undo hers for the benefit of your humble servant; I have never had such a time in my life, and we were just going to make arrangements to meet again when somebody she knew had the bad taste to get in at the last station but one."

James Grieve is much more liberal in his translation. He doesn't even try to make a pun on girdle, or zone, but simply has Bloch getting "a nice ride": "Well, anyway," he said, "you deserve to be congratulated—she must have given you a nice time. I had just met her a few days before, you see, riding on the suburban line. She had no objection to yours truly, and so a nice ride was had by one and all, and we were just on the point of arranging to do it again, on a future occasion, when someone she knew had the bad form to get on, just one stop before the terminus."

In general, I like the liberties Grieve takes with the text. I will never read the book in French, so I don't need a "trot" (do students still use that term?); what I want is an English-language equivalent of what Proust wrote in the opening decades of the last century. Still, there is one instance in which he quite mangles one of my favorite passages, which I underlined some forty years ago. As Scott Moncrieff phrased it: "It is one of the systems of hygiene among which we are at liberty to choose our own, a system which is perhaps not to be recommended too strongly, but it gives us a certain tranquillity with which to spend what remains of life, and also—since it enables us to regret nothing, by assuring us that we have attained to the best, and that the best was nothing out of the common—with which to resign ourselves to death."

The best was nothing out of the common! A pretty phrase, though I would have rendered it "nothing out of the ordinary." Grieve falls far short, in my opinion: "therein lies one of the modes of mental hygiene available to us, which, though it may not be the most recommendable, can certainly afford us a measure of equanimity for getting through life and—since it enables us to have no regrets, by assuring us that we have had the best of things, and that the best of things was not up to much— of resigning us to death."

Recommendable? Equanimity? Good grief.

Remembering the past

As suggested by its title, memory is a major theme of *In Search of Lost Time*. Proust's understanding of memory is clearly stated in this second volume: "the greater part of our memory lies outside us, in a dampish breeze, in the musty air of a bedroom or the smell of autumn's first fires, things through which we can retrieve any part of us that the reasoning mind . . . disdained, the last vestige of the past, the best of it, the part which, after all our tears have dried, can make us weep again. Outside us? Inside us, more like, but stored away. . . . It is only because we have forgotten that we can now and then return to the person we once were, envisage things as that person did, be hurt again, because we are not ourselves anymore, but someone else, who once loved something that we no longer care about."

This is what Roger Shattuck calls Proust's "binocular vision." The crumb of madeleine dipped in an herbal tea does not actually return us to the past: we bring the separation with us, and it is this double vision that makes the experience so poignant.

Gotcha!

On page 95 of the Viking edition, Swann is playing games with his wife's guest-list, and he proposes to add Dr. Cottard and his wife to the circle of those invited to dinner. Madame Bontemps (who by the way is Albertine's aunt) is horrified. Previously she had gloated over her inclusion at the expense of the Cottards. "Would she even have the heart to tell her own husband that Professor Cottard and his wife were not to partake of the very pleasure she had assured him was unique to themselves?" *Not* of course is a typo for *now*, an error that reverses the meaning of the sentence—indeed, of two full pages in which Proust revels in Swann's warped sense of humor.

10

The translator

James Grieve no doubt came to Penguin's attention because in 1982 he rendered *A Search for Lost Time: Swann's Way* for Australian National University. Mine is a paperback edition, and it's rather hard to find, at least if you don't live in Australia. However, you can get the flavor from my chapter on the "dueling madeleines," a bit later in this book.

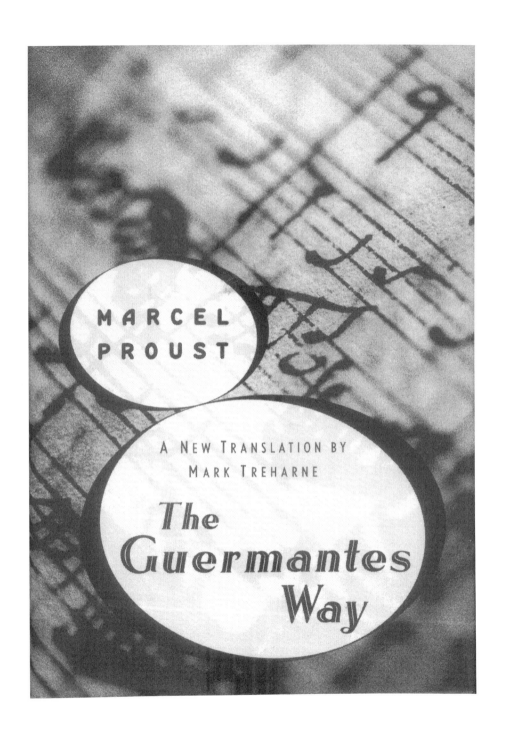

MARCEL
PROUST

A New Translation by
Mark Treharne

The
Guermantes
Way

3 – *The Guermantes Way*

In French: *Le Côté de Guermantes*

The two-minute *Guermantes*

Marcel's family moves to the sprawl of apartments making up the Hôtel de Guermantes. Thus granted almost daily sightings of the Duchesse de Guermantes, Marcel—of course!—falls in love with her. Hoping for an introduction, he visits her nephew, Robert de Saint-Loup, at the barracks in Doncières. Instead, they go to the theater with Saint-Loup's beloved (Rachel, whom we met earlier as a twenty-franc whore) and Marcel gets an invitation to the second-rate salon of the Marquise de Villeparisis, where he renews his acquaintance with the Baron de Charlus. (All these except Rachel are members of the Guermantes clan.)

His grandmother dies, and, almost immediately. Albertine comes back into his life. Since he doesn't care one way or another, he promptly succeeds in bedding her, though it's unclear whether this involves anything beyond heavy petting. The Duchesse too, now that he's not infatuated with her, takes him up. Charlus, however, is a different matter. Marcel can't quite figure him out!

Exploring the ways of society

In this, the least compelling part of Proust's novel, he further explores his peculiar conception of physical love, which in his view is never reciprocated. The man is an infatuated pursuer, squandering time, wealth, and reputation on a woman who consumes them all while casting her own glances on lesser beings: in this case, Saint-Loup as the pursuer and Rachel as the pursued. On this whore whom at an earlier time he could have hired for twenty francs, Saint-Loup spends a fortune that Marcel estimates to be a million francs. (Very roughly, one franc at the turn of the 20th Century equates to one or two U.S. dollars at the turn of the 21st.) In one of Proust's neat transformations, however, Rachel has meanwhile turned out to be a talented actress.

There follows an astonishing tour de force at the home of the Marquise de Villeparisis, where for some hundred pages we are immersed in a Dickensian comedy of society. The love of Saint-Loup for Rachel is an echo of Swann's for Odette; so too does the marquise's salon remind us of Madame Verdurin's, where Swann's love affair played out. Unusual for him, Proust pokes us in the eye with the comparison: a few days later, Young Marcel takes his grandmother for a stroll on the Champs Élysées, where she is taken ill. She retreats to the public toilets, and Marcel is left to listen to the frumpy woman who presides over these facilities, and who explains to the groundsman that not everyone is welcome into her "parlors." She's a stand-in for Madame Verdurin, for the Marquise de Villeparisis, and (ultimately) for the Duchesse de Guermantes herself.

Indeed, once we get to know her, the beautiful and brilliant Duchesse is no more to be admired than Madame Verdurin, whom Proust mocked so mercilessly in *Swann's Way*. Marcel's maiden visit to her salon actually takes considerably more than a hundred pages to describe; the result is hardly flattering to this seeming pinnacle of society. The book ends in another Dickensian scene: Marcel and the ailing Charles Swann happen to be visiting the Duc and Duchesse just before they are to go out to a ball. The Duchesse wants Swann to travel with them to Venice; he demurs; she insists; he explains that he is incurably ill, and that by the time they leave he will be dead. The aristocratic couple simply don't want to hear it, and instead get into an uproar because she proves to be wearing black shoes with a red dress. They will serve, she says. The Duc will have none of it. Having just assured Swann that they were in a terrible hurry, and that the dying man will outlive them all, he now declares that there is plenty of time for the Duchesse to swap the black shoes for her red ones.

The translation

Mark Treharne follows the example set by James Grieve, translating *la petite bande* as "the little gang." But he's not nearly so slangy, and overall he steers a middle course between Scott Moncrieff and Lydia Davis, who did such a nice job with *Swann's Way*. Here, for example, Scott Moncrieff translates an amusing sentence about the style with which members of the Guermantes clan greet a stranger:

"At the moment when a Guermantes, were he no more than twenty, but treading already in the footsteps of his ancestors, heard your name uttered by the person who introduced you, he let fall on you as though he had by no means made up his mind to say 'How d'ye do?' a gaze generally blue, always of the coldness of a steel blade which he seemed ready to plunge into the deepest recesses of your heart."

Treharne's version isn't radically different, but how much more smoothly it flows:

"The moment he heard your name uttered by the person introducing you, a Guermantes, even a twenty-year-old Guermantes, but treading already in the footsteps of his elders, let fall against you, as though he had not made up to mind to acknowledge you, a gaze that was generally blue and always as cold as a steel blade, seemingly destined to plunge into the deepest recesses of your heart."

That the concluding phrases are identical is no accident. Treharne concludes his introduction to *The Guermantes Way* by saying: "I should, finally, like to acknowledge my debt to the Moncrieff / Kilmartin edition revised by D. J. Enright. I have worked very much in the shadow of these previous translators and with much gratitude toward them."

MARCEL
PROUST

Sodom
and
Gomorrah

A New Translation by
John Sturrock

4 – *Sodom and Gomorrah*

In French: *Sodome et Gomorrhe*
Also translated as: *Cities of the Plain*

The two-minute *Sodom*

Marcel spies on an encounter between the Baron de Charlus and a tailor named Jupien, after which he goes to a *soirée* at the Princesse de Guermantes's. Returning home, he expects a routine midnight visit from Albertine, and is put into a fever of lust and suspicion when she is slow to appear.

He then returns for a season at Balbec. Albertine is staying nearby, and continues to demonstrate her usual astonishing freedom of action (for a young woman at the turn of the 20th Century). By being available to Marcel, but not committed entirely to him, Albertine enslaves him in the usual Proustian fashion.

Also nearby are the awful Verdurins. Like Swann before them, Marcel and Charlus join the "little clan" for their private reasons, which sets off another of Proust's hilarious hundred-page *salon* scenes. Madame Verdurin has recently inherited a few million francs, which will lubricate her ascent into society. This woman is so terrible that you find yourself cheering the baron as he jousts with her.

Of high society, memory, and sexuality

One of the recurring themes in Proust's novel is the interplay among the select invitees at one or another Paris salon. In *Swann's Way*, the salon belongs to Madame Verurdin, whose "little clan" includes a young painter (who later morphs into the genius Elstir, based perhaps on Whistler), a foolish doctor (who turns out to be a great diagnostician), and other luminaries who age and evolve throughout the novel. In *The Guermantes Way*, we move into more distinguished

17

circles, first at the Marquise de Villeparisis's, then at the Duchesse de Guermantes's. And here, in *Sodom and Gomorrah*, we reach the very highest of Parisian high society: a *soirée* at the Princesse de Guermantes's. But Proust is not content merely to climb the ladder. Just as his characters rise and descend—and rise again, like Sisyphus pushing the stone up the hill through all eternity—so do the salons rise and fall. I don"t think I am betraying a confidence by revealing that the beautiful Duchesse will be cast down as a result of her own bad behavior, while the awful Madame Verurdin will rise in the world thanks to her great wealth.

When Marcel (he is now about twenty-one) returns to Balbec for the season, he is overwhelmed with grief for his grandmother, whose death was detailed in *The Guermantes Way*, but whom at the time he mourned only in perfunctory fashion. Now he sees the wall that, several years earlier, had separated him from his grandmother, and upon which they had been accustomed to tap messages to one another. As with "voluntary" and "involuntary" memory, so it is with voluntary and in-voluntary grief: triggered by the sight of the wall, Marcel realizes for the first time what he has lost:

"I knew that now I could knock, more loudly even, that nothing could again wake her, that I would not hear any response, that my grandmother would never again come. And I asked nothing more of God, if there is a paradise, than to be able to give there the three little taps on that partition that my grandmother would recognize anywhere, and to which she would respond with those other taps that meant, 'Don't fret yourself, little mouse, I realize you're impatient, but I'm just coming,' and that he should let me remain with her for all eternity, which would not be too long for the two of us."

Was ever grief more beautifully expressed?

Soon, however, grief is forgotten and Marcel is once again sniffing about the "young girls in flower" who infatuated him in the novel's second volume. There are two mysteries here: the nature of the sexual relations between these people; and their gender. As to the first, it is never entirely clear to me whether Marcel actually gets it on with his "girls." He claims at one point that he enjoyed "moments of pleasure" with, and was "granted their fragile favors" by, *no less than fourteen young women* during this second summer at Balbec. These girls know one another, they are scarcely twenty years old, they come from upper-middle-class families—and Queen Victoria is still on her throne! Marcel would have done quite well, it seems to me, if he had succeeded in *kissing* fourteen girls that summer.

Of the fourteen, Albertine Simonet is his beloved. Marcel suspects her of hankering after women, and he sees every woman who comes to Balbec as a likely bedmate for her. Was female homosexuality really so rampant in turn-of-the-century France? As earlier with Gilberte Swann, his relations with Albertine often seem easier to understand if we take off the feminine ending: a pretty young man named Albert could certainly come and go through the Balbec nights, and if the lover suspected him of *hetereosexual* tendencies, then he might have reason to fear the arrival of each new woman. (The girl who most often makes a third with Marcel and Albertine also has an ambivalent name: Andrée.)

Altogether, this is my favorite of the Penguin Proust translations thus far. A wonderfully funny study of society, if not of sex!

British v. American editions

In my determination to own hardcover copies of all six books of the new translations, I managed to double up on *Sodom and Gomorrah*, so I'm able to compare the British edition (Allen Lane, 2002) with the American (Viking, 2004). Viking's *Sodom* is much more handsome: the pages are larger, and they're stitched instead of glued to the backing. The dark gray dustcover stands up better to handling than Allen Lane's mostly black jacket, which already shows my fingerprints after very little use. Viking's cloth cover, too, strikes me as more distinguished.

There are the expected small differences in usage: hair-colour becomes hair color; theatre becomes theater. The most dramatic change, however, is the treatment of literary quotations: in the Allen Lane edition, Samson is quoted as saying *"Les duex sexes mourront chacon de son côté,"* with a translation in the chapter notes; Viking renders the quote as "The two sexes will die each on its own side" and banishes the *French* to the back of the book. Being the typical

19

monophone American, I prefer Viking's treatment. (The Kindle e-book editions of the Penguin Proust are the Allen Lane versions.)

Gotcha!

I was trained to use the possessive before a gerund, so I winced at this phrase on page 121: "I don't understand Basin letting her talk" (instead of *Basin's*, as Scott Moncrieff rendered it, and as I would have done). But John Sturrock is not consistent: on page 165, he reverts to the old ways: "I can understand its annoying you . . . ." Why not *it*?

A similar small barbarism: on page 446, Sturrock has Proust writing that Charlus was doing his best to *try and please* Morel. Somehow, I don't think Proust would have liked that phrasing! It should be *try to please*, thank you very much.

Here's a typo on page 260: "these common travelers would have been less interested than I was had—despite the notoriety some had acquired. . . ." This is one of Proust's many-layered sentences, and there should be a comma after *was*. The British edition gets it right (and of course there's a double *l* in travelers).

Here's a *gotcha!* that must be laid at Proust's door: on page 360, Madame Verdurin says to Marcel, speaking of Charles Swann as a member of her circle "he was very fond of you, for that matter; he spoke about you in a delightful way. . . ." But Marcel hadn't yet been born when Swann was exiled from the Verdurins' circle. Odette, as his wife, occasionally received Madame Verdurin, but there is no indication that Swann ever went to the Verdurins' after his marriage.

And another: on page 393, the narrator muses that the towns around Balbec are "like an officer in my regiment." But this is supposed to be Marcel speaking, and he (unlike Proust) has never been in the army. (Page numbers for the Viking edition.)

THE PRISONER AND THE FUGITIVE

MARCEL PROUST

5 – *The Prisoner*

In French: *La Prisonnière*
Also translated as: *The Captive*

The two-minute *Prisoner*

Albertine has come to Paris and moved in with Marcel, whose parents are conveniently absent. Charlus and Morel (who come to the Hôtel de Guermantes to see Jupien's niece, whom Morel is more or less engaged to marry) are part of his daily routine, as is the Duchesse de Guermantes, who dispenses advice on what clothes Marcel should buy for "your friend." Nobody—not Françoise, the super-judgmental servant; not Madame Bontemps, Albertine's aunt and guardian—seems to think it's the least bit odd that the girl should be living there with him.

Noticing that Albertine wants to visit the Verdurins, Marcel jockeys her into staying home, and himself pays a visit to the salon, which Charlus and Morel are also to attend. The awful *Patronne* is inexorably rising in society through her ability to attract artists like Anatole France, Igor Stravinsky, and Richard Strauss. The baron is abetting her ambition, and has invited (page 223) "two dukes, an eminent general, a famous writer, great doctor and distinguished lawyer" (and a bunch of others, including the Queen of Naples) to this particular evening. Alas, they treat Charlus as their host, ignoring Madame Verdurin. Her revenge is swift and terrible: she turns Morel against the baron, who is crushed to the point of physical collapse.

Marcel goes home, suffering torments of jealousy because he has learned that Albertine has been lying to him about her friendships with some notorious lesbians. He writhes about this for eighty pages, until one morning he wakes up and—serve him bloody well right! —finds her gone.

Of love & jealousy, boys & girls

Time and again, Proust tells us of a tragi-comic love affair, in which the male (Swann, Marcel, Saint-Loup, and now again Marcel) squanders time, emotion, and wealth upon a female (Odette, Gilberte, Rachel, and now Albertine) who couldn't care less for him, and for the most part is in it only for the money. (Perhaps significantly, because she's based on an actual girl with whom Proust had boyishly been in love, Gilberte is somewhat an exception to this rule. She's a good kid; she just doesn't happen to fancy Marcel.) The torments suffered by these men do certainly invoke our young loves: most of us have experienced such moments of despair. Yet Proust never seems to have gone beyond them to a mutually satisfactory affair—let alone marriage! His characters are stuck forever at the stage of infatuation, in which the more deeply we love, the more cruel and less affectionate the beloved becomes.

I suspect that this is because Proust's loves were mostly unconsummated. In *The Prisoner*, this aspect of the Marcel-Albertine affair is stated explicitly on page 84: "Albertine always alarmed me when she said that I was quite right to protect her reputation by saying that I was not her lover, since, as she said, 'you aren't, are you, not really.' Perhaps I was not, in the complete sense, but was I to think that she did with other men all the things we did together, only to say she had not been their mistress?" A good cuddle and a bit of lubrication—that seems to have been Proust's idea of sexual love.

Even better if the beloved isn't awake! On pages 60-62, he writes: "I listened to . . . the sound of her sleep. So long as it continued I could dream of her and look at her at the same time, and when her sleep became deeper, touch her and kiss her. . . . The sound of Albertine's breathing, growing louder, could almost have been mistaken for the breathlessness of pleasure, and as my own pleasure neared completion, I could kiss her without breaking into her sleep. It seemed to me at these moments that I possessed her more completely, like an unconscious and unresisting part of dumb nature."

So Proust's novel-within-a-novel is not so much the story of a homosexual man as of an impotent one. This comes out very clearly in the *casser le pot* episode, when Albertine (page 311) lets slip that she'd like to go out and "get broken" (*me faire casser*)—what?—"my jar" (*le pot*), as Marcel finally completes the sentence. *Casser le pot* was French slang for rear-window sex, and doesn't make a whole lot of sense unless Albertine were actually Albert. If Marcel's sweetie were a man, and Marcel weren't an effective lover, then the beloved might well regret hanging around the apartment night after night, when he could go out and get himself properly buggered.

As a result of this disconnection, Proust's accounts of affairs between men and women often seem unreal to me, or perhaps I should say *surreal*, except when they evoke my own Charlie Brown days. ("I saw the red-haired girl today. . . . I couldn't think what to say to her. So I hit her!")

Even creepier is Marcel's formula of love and rejection. When Albertine behaves, he doesn't particularly like her; when she strays, his infatuation flames up again. Page 21: "Every day I found her less pretty. Only the desire which she excited in others, when I learned of it and began to suffer again, in my desire to keep her from them, could put her back on her pedestal. Suffering alone gave life to my tedious attachment to her. When she disappeared, taking with her the need to alleviate my pain, which demanded all my attention like some dreadful hobby, I realized how little she meant to me—as little, no doubt, as I meant to her."

British and (no!) American edition

The Prisoner and *The Fugitive* are often bound together as a single volume, and the Penguin Proust follows this tradition. The first book of the "Albertine cycle" was translated by Carol Clark. Alas, it and the next two books have fallen afoul of American copyright law, which (thanks to the late Sonny Bono) insanely protects literary works for ninety-five years after the author's death. The first four books of Proust's great novel were published during his lifetime, so they fell into the public domain before the rock star and California congressman could spoil our enjoyment. The last three, however, are "protected" by the Sono Bono Law—also called the Mickey Mouse Provision, since its real intent was to protect the Disney Studios' interest in its odious mouse. Viking tells me that it won't publish these books until 2018!

However, the British paperbacks (except for their covers, identical to the Allen Lane editions) are imported to the U.S. under the Penguin imprint, both in print editions and as e-books.

Marcel and the Narrator

I've always thought of the central character in *Lost Time* as Little Marcel. On page 64 of *The Prisoner*, there's a hint that this is indeed the case. Writing of Albertine's awakening in the narrator's bed, Proust writes: "Now she began to speak; her first words were 'darling' or 'my darling,' followed by my Christian name, which, if we give the narrator the same name as the author of this book, would produce 'darling Marcel' or 'my darling Marcel'." Apparently Proust liked the effect, because on page 140 he has Albertine beginning a note to the narrator with "My dear darling Marcel" and ending it "Oh Marcel, Marcel! Your very own Albertine."

Gotcha!

The Prisoner was the first book of the novel to be published after Proust's death, and he was working on it (and the two that follow) until he died. So it is naturally rougher than the earlier books, with many small solecisms and contradictions that he would have corrected had he lived a year or two longer. Thus, in one of his spasms of lust, Marcel spots a blonde dairy-girl whom he invites up to his room under the pretext that he needs her to carry a letter for him. As soon as he sees her up close, of course, he loses interest in the project and sends her packing with a five-franc tip. That's on page 132; by page 136, the tip has been reduced to a mere two francs.

I briefly thought I'd found a typographical error when I saw the word *appal* on page 361, only to learn that this is the preferred British spelling of *appall*.

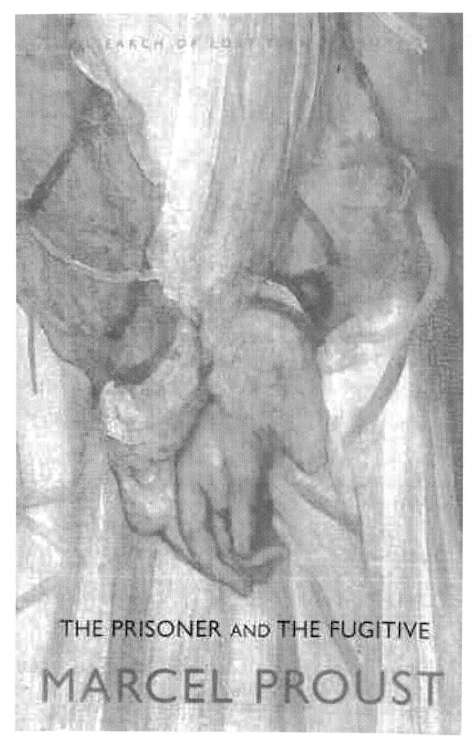

6 – *The Fugitive*

In French: *La Fugitive, Albertine disparue*
Also translated as: *The Sweet Cheat Gone, Albertine Gone*

The two-minute *Fugitive*

Marcel dispatches Robert de Saint-Loup to offer Albertine's aunt 30,000 francs if she can persuade the fugitive to return. More directly, he tells Albertine that he had ordered a yacht and a Rolls for her; what a pity they won't be used! And he plays the jealousy card by suggesting that Andrée could replace her. (He never thinks to say: "I love you. Please come back!") Alas, the next news he gets is from the aunt, telling him that Albertine was killed in a fall from her horse. This sets Marcel off on a hundred-page revel in the metaphysics of grief.

He knows he's healing when he sees a provocative blonde in the street and sets out to learn her name: Forcheville. She proves to be his childhood sweetheart, Gilberte Swann, whose mother has remarried the impoverished nobleman who was sniffing about her in *Swann's Way*, and who as part of the deal adopted Gilberte. Marcel then does take up with Andrée, who spins all sorts of lurid stories about the dead girl, some of them involving the violinist Morel.

Marcel and his mother make his long-delayed pilgrimage to Venice, and Gilberte marries Saint-Loup—who like almost every character in the novel is now revealed to be a homosexual. Marcel visits Madame de Saint-Loup at Tansonville and learns, among other things, that when he first spied her on those premises as a boy, the gesture she flipped him wasn't a dismissal but an invitation to the ball.

On grief and jealousy

As when Marcel grieves for his grandmother on his second visit to Balbec, Proust never writes so compellingly as when the subject is loss. Here he is (pages 477-478) yearning for Albertine: "My imagination

27

sought her in the skies, on evenings like those when we were still able to gaze at it together; I tried to wing my affections towards her, beyond the moonlight that she loved, to console her for no longer being alive, and this love for a person who had become so remote was like a religion, my thoughts rose towards her like prayers."

Less moving, but no less brilliant, is the way (page 554) he shows grief receding. The Duchesse de Guermantes invites him to the opera. "But I replied sadly: 'No, I cannot go to the theatre, I have lost a friend. She was very dear to me.' The tears nearly came to my eyes as I said it and yet for the first time I felt something akin to pleasure in talking about it. It was from that moment that I started to write to everyone to tell them of my great sorrow and to cease to feel it." That cuts fairly close to the bone!

Because it was never finally reviewed by Proust, *The Fugitive* too is rough in spots, but also revealing. In the earlier books, I felt that the characters were younger than the conventional wisdom would have them. In *In the Shadow of Young Girls in Flower*, Marcel and the girls are generally thought to be eighteen, but here Marcel refers to the Albertine of that era (page 469) as "appearing to me at the moment of puberty," which is more or less how I placed all of them at Balbec— i.e., in their very early teens. (Later, to be sure, he suggests that they were sixteen.)

The biographer Ronald Hayman tells us that Proust intended to cut 250 pages from this already-short book, and to change its title from *La Fugitive* to *Albertine disparue*. The re-titling was done, but his post-humous editors Robert Proust and Jacques Rivière ignored the cuts in the edition published in 1925. "It is clear," Hayman writes, "that what [Proust] had in mind was whole volumes to be interpolated between *Albertine disparue* and *Le Temps retrouvé*." (Whole volumes, *mon dieu!*) In the truncated book, Albertine runs off to join her lesbian friends, thus mooting much of Marcel's ponderings about this element of her nature; she dies on the bank of the Vivonne in Combray, instead of in Touraine; and the chapter about Albertine and Andrée is jettisoned.

The Penguin Proust

Well into volume five, I am no longer conscious that I am reading a new translation, nor that I am in the hands of seven different translators; I'm simply reading for pleasure.

I mentioned earlier that the British editions leave Proust's literary quotations in French, with an English translation in the notes, while the American editions do just the opposite. This didn't trouble me until I came to pages 426-427 of the *Prisoner / Fugitive* volume, where five quotations from Racine appear in the same long paragraph. I found this a bit irritating: if my French is insufficient to allow me to read Proust in the original, why should the editors assume that I can read Racine?

The Gotcha! below gave me a reason to compare the old and new translations. In *The Sweet Cheat Gone*, Scott Moncrieff writes as follows: "Associated now with the memory of my love, Albertine's physical and social attributes, in spite of which I had loved her, attracted my desire on the contrary towards what at one time it would least readily have chosen: dark girls of the lower middle class."

Which Peter Collier renders: "Now that they were associated with the memory of my love, the physical and social attributes of Albertine, whom I had loved in spite of them, had the opposite effect, that of orientating my desire towards what previously it would have least naturally have chosen, dark-haired girls from the lower-middle classes." Much smoother, I think.

Gotcha!

Oh, good grief! In the quote above (page 518), Mr. Collier has Marcel say *orientating*. This is particularly funny since the verb comes from the French *orienter*, not *orientater*. Remembering that I got caught with the British spelling of appal in *The Prisoner*, I immediately went to the *Shorter Oxford*, and as I suspected, *orientate* appears there only as an alternate spelling of the verb *orient*, with the notation that it is probably a "back-form" from *orientation*. I detest these superfluous syllables. Why would anyone say *orientate* for *orient*, or *preventative* for *preventive*? I am sure that Proust would not have been so sloppy!

Which is not to say he was never sloppy: in *Swann's Way*, Gilberte is a redhead, but in *The Fugitive* she is blonde (and remembered as a blonde).

Swann's Way, Guermantes Way

When Gilberte married Saint-Loup, the two "ways" of Marcel's boyhood are joined. And when Marcel goes to Tansonville to visit Madame de Saint-Loup, he is astonished to have her tell him that the "ways" are actually one and the same: "Gilberte said: 'If you like, we could still go out one afternoon to walk towards Guermantes, but we could walk past Méséglise [i.e., Swann's way], it's the prettiest route,' a sentence which overturned all the ideas of my childhood by revealing that the two ways were not as irreconcilable as I had thought."

IN SEARCH OF LOST TIME   VOLUME 6

FINDING TIME AGAIN

MARCEL PROUST

7 – Finding Time Again

In French: *Le Temps retrouvé*
Also translated as: *The Past Recaptured, Time Regained*

The two-minute *Finding Time*

Marcel learns more about Gilberte's childhood affection for him, and of her husband's adult yearning for men. Between times he reads a fictionalized section from the *Goncourt Journals*, dealing with the wonders of the Verdurin salon (wonders that have escaped Marcel, as indeed they have escaped us).

Flash forward to the war. Combray (and Tansonville, with Gilberte in it) is a battlefield; in Paris, the Baron de Charlus loses the regard of society even as Madame Verdurin gains it. Marcel meanwhile spends long periods in the sanatorium, whether for his asthma or his mental health, returning only for visits. In the final one of these, he attends a *soirée* at the Prince de Guermantes's. En route, he meets a decrepit Baron de Charlus, in the care of Jupien the former tailor, then is barraged by moments from his past.

At the Prince's party, Marcel is bombarded with examples of "involuntary memory," which cause him to reflect upon life, art, and society. He is also astonished to discover that everyone has grown old (and so, presumably, has he). Gilberte looks like her mother, and her daughter is all but grown. "I thought she was very beautiful: still full of hopes, laughing, formed out of the very years I had lost, she looked like my youth" (page 342). Indeed, there's a hint that Marcel will add the never-named young woman to his menagerie of young girls in flower—and that with her mother's approval!

At the end of all, Marcel resolves to write the novel that has been bugging him for most of the last thousand pages: "And I understood that all these raw materials for a literary work were actually my past life; I understood that they had come to me, in frivolous pleasures, in idleness, in tenderness, in sorrow, that they had been stored up by me

32

without my divining their ultimate purpose, . . . any more than a seed does as it lays up a reserve of all the nutrients which will feed the plant. Like the seed, I would be able to die when the plant had developed, and I began to see that I had lived for its sake without knowing it."

The Penguin Proust

It's extraordinary how *Swann's Way* (published in 1913, before the following books were written) prefigures the end of Proust's sprawling novel. As Gilberte writes of their childhood haunts (page 64): "They now share the same immortal fame as Austerliz or Valmy. The battle of Méséglise lasted for more than eight months, in the course of which the Germans lost six hundred thousand men and destroyed Méséglise, but they did not take it. . . . The French blew up the little bridge over the Vivonne . . . the Germans put up some new ones, and for the last year and a half they have held one half of Combray and the French have held the other." It's as if Proust had foreseen the First World War as a necessary bookend to his novel.

The evening at the Prince de Guermantes's is the last, the longest, and I'm sorry to say the least gripping of Proust's soirée scenes. He takes more than fifty pages from the dooryard to the ballroom, and more than two hundred pages in the room itself.

More than in the six volumes that precede it, we are made aware that Proust is a philosopher as much as he is a novelist. I have to strain to follow his aesthetics, but his study of memory (which undergirds the entire novel, from the cake dipped in herbal tea in *Swann's Way* to the multiple flashes of "involuntary memory" in *Finding Time Again*) is more accessible. "The only true paradise is a paradise we have lost," he writes (page 179). And we can re-enter that paradise not by attempting to recall it, but "for the duration of a flash of lightning" by encountering a physical sensation (the clink of a fork that recalls a workman's hammer, the uneven paving stones in front of the Prince de Guermantes's house that duplicate those in front of St. Mark's in Venice, the starched napkin evoking those at the Grand Hotel in Balbec) that enables us to live simultaneously in the past and in the present: "a little bit of time in its pure state" (page 180). Thus the intensity of the pleasure Marcel experienced when he tasted the moistened tea-cake. For a moment, he actually exists both in the past and the present: "Even if the simple taste of a madeleine does not seem logically to contain reasons for this joy, we can understand how the word 'death' has no meaning for him; situated outside of time, what should he fear from the future?" (page 180). (The page references are to the Allen Lane hardcover.)

Gotcha!

Like the other posthumously published books, *Finding Time Again* is marred by occasional solecisms that Proust doubtless would have corrected if he had lived a year or two longer. Some of this is deliberate: "Some music-lovers find that, orchestrated by X——, the music of Z—— becomes absolutely different. . . ." Proust just never got around to filling in these literal blanks. Others are more awkward: on page 304, we are suddenly treated to a scene at the home of the aged actress La Berma—a scene that Marcel couldn't possibly have witnessed, and that serves as a four-page interruption to the Prince's party. In the course of it, he carelessly swaps the genders of La Berma's daughter and son-in-law, so that for a moment they are her son and daughter-in-law.

Dueling Madeleines

The most famous words Proust ever wrote are those in which he recalled how the taste of a little cake, dipped in tea, brought his childhood back to him entire. Here are five versions of that passage, moving backwards from Lydia Davis's translation for Penguin—to the Modern Library collaboration of D. J. Enright, Terence Kilmartin, and Charles Scott Moncrieff—to James Grieve's version for Australian National University—to Scott Moncrieff's original translation—to what Proust actually wrote, with the crucial sentence put in boldface type:

Lydia Davis (2003)

For many years already, everything about Combray that was not the theatre and drama of my bedtime had ceased to exist for me, when one day in winter, as I came home, my mother, seeing that I was cold, suggested that, contrary to my habit, I have a little tea. I refused at first and then, I do not know why, changed my mind. She sent for one of those squat, plump cakes called petites madeleines that look as though they have been molded in the grooved valve of a scallop-shell. And soon, mechanically, oppressed by the gloomy day and the prospect of a sad future, I carried to my lips a spoonful of the tea in which I had let soften a piece of madeleine. **But at the very instant when the mouthful of tea mixed with cake-crumbs touched my palate, I quivered, attentive to the extraordinary thing that was happening in me. A delicious pleasure had invaded me, isolated me, without my having any notion as to its cause.** It had immediately made the vicissitudes of life unimportant to me, its disasters innocuous, its brevity illusory, acting in the same way that love acts, by filling me with a precious essence: or rather this essence was not in me, it was me.

D. J. Enright et al (1992)

Many years had elapsed during which nothing of Combray, except what lay in the theatre and the drama of my going to bed there, had any existence for me, when one day in winter, on my return home, my mother, seeing that I was cold, offered me some tea, a thing I did not ordinarily take. I declined at first, and then, for no particular reason, changed my mind. She sent for one of those squat, plump little cakes called "petites madeleines", which look as though they had been moulded in the fluted valve of a scallop shell. And soon, mechanically, dispirited after a dreary day with the prospect of a depressing morrow, I raised to my lips a spoonful of the tea in which I had soaked a morsel of the cake. **No sooner had the warm liquid mixed with the crumbs touched my palate than a shiver ran through me and I stopped, intent upon the extraordinary thing that was happening to me. An exquisite pleasure had invaded my senses, something isolated, detached, with no suggestion of its origin.** And at once the vicissitudes of life had become indifferent to me, its disasters innocuous, its brevity illusory—this new sensation having had the effect, which love has, of filling me with a precious essence; or rather this essence was not in me, it was me.

James Grieve (1982)

One winter's day, years after Combray had shrunk to the mere stage-set for my bedtime performance, I came home cold and my mother suggested I have a cup of tea, a thing I did not usually do. My first impulse was to decline; then for some reason I changed my mind. My mother sent for one of those dumpy little sponge-cakes called *madeleines*, which look as though they have been moulded inside a corrugated scallop-shell. Soon, depressed by the gloomy day and the promise of more like it to come, I took a mechanical sip at a spoonful of tea with a piece of the cake soaked in it. **But at the very moment when the sip of tea and cake-crumbs touched my palate, a thrill ran through me and I immediately focussed my attention on something strange happening inside me. I had been suddenly singled out**

and filled with a sweet feeling of joy, although I had no inkling of where it had come from. The joy had instantly made me indifferent to the vicissitudes of life, inoculated me against any setback it might have in store and shown me that its brevity was an irrelevant illusion; it had acted on me as love acts, filling me with a precious essence—or rather, the essence was not put into me, it was me, I was it.

Scott Moncrieff (1922)

Many years had elapsed during which nothing of Combray, save what was comprised in the theatre and the drama of my going to bed there, had any existence for me, when one day in winter, as I came home, my mother, seeing that I was cold, offered me some tea, a thing I did not ordinarily take. I declined at first, and then, for no particular reason, changed my mind. She sent out for one of those short, plump little cakes called 'petites madeleines,' which look as though they had been moulded in the fluted scallop of a pilgrim's shell. And soon, mechanically, weary after a dull day with the prospect of a depressing morrow, I raised to my lips a spoonful of the tea in which I had soaked a morsel of the cake. **No sooner had the warm liquid, and the crumbs with it, touched my palate than a shudder ran through my whole body, and I stopped, intent upon the extraordinary changes that were taking place. An exquisite pleasure had invaded my senses, but individual, detached, with no suggestion of its origin.** And at once the vicissitudes of life had become indifferent to me, its disasters innocuous, its brevity illusory—this new sensation having had on me the effect which love has of filling me with a precious essence; or rather this essence was not in me, it was myself.

Marcel Proust (1913)

Il y avait déjà bien des années que, de Combray, tout ce qui n'était pas le théâtre et la drame de mon coucher, n'existait plus pour moi, quand un jour d'hiver, comme je rentrais à la maison, ma mère, voyant que j'avais froid, me proposa de me faire prendre, contre mon habitude, un peu de thé. Je refusai d'abord et, je ne sais pourquoi, me ravisai. Elle envoya chercher un de ces gâteaux courts et dodus appelés Petites Madeleines qui semblaient avoir été moulés dans la valve rainurée d'une coquille de Saint-Jacques. Et bientôt, machinalement, accablé par la morne journée et la perspective d'un triste lendemain, je portai à mes lèvres une cuillerée du thé où j'avais laissé s'amollir un morceau de madeleine. **Mais à l'instant même où la gorgée mêlée des miettes du gâteau toucha mon palais, je tressaillis, attentif à ce qui se passait d'extraordinaire en moi. Un plaisir délicieux m'avait envahi, isolé, sans la notion de sa cause.** Il m'avait aussitôt rendu les vicissitudes de la vie indifférentes, ses désastres inoffensifs, sa brièveté illusoire, de la même façon qu'opère l'amour, en me remplissant d'une essence précieuse: ou plutôt cette essence n'était pas en moi, elle était moi.

The Love of His Life

The most important character in Proust's novel is Albertine Simonet, who first appears in *Young Girls in Flower* as an elusive member of the "little gang" of girls at the seashore. When Marcel visits Albertine's hotel bedroom and tries to kiss her, she defeats him by threatening to ring the service bell. In *The Guermantes Way*, the situations are reversed: she visits *his* bedroom, and he easily gets it on with her—but not to coitus, I suspect. At this point, he's jolly young Alfred E. Neuman himself: "What, me worry?" This situation likewise reverses itself: in *Sodom and Gomorrah*, Marcel becomes a slave to Albertine, who says like Carmen: "If you love me, I don't love you!" This situation leads us into the next two books of the novel, which are more or less devoted to the love-duel between Marcel and Albertine.

When Proust began his novel, he envisioned it as a two-volume work, which soon became three. As he wrote on and on, he went back to the earlier (but still unpublished) volumes and added material to them, so they in turn became longer. This process was abetted by the turmoil of the First World War, when his publisher was called to service and the company closed down. *Swann's Way* appeared in 1913, but there was a five-year lapse before *Young Girls* was published, with the others following at roughly two-year intervals. In addition to building Albertine into a central character, Proust incorporated the war into his novel.

Marcel's relationship with Albertine is based largely upon Proust's with Alfred Agostinelli. An occasional chauffeur from the summer of 1907, he also served as companion to his lonely employer, playing checkers and otherwise entertaining him. (Proust was drawn to lower-class companions, usually men, though he formed the same sort of relationship with women servants like Céleste Albaret, his housekeeper for many years.) In an essay for *Figaro* that November, Proust put on display his love for the modern age and also for his "mechanic," and an astonishing presentiment that machinery would be the death of him: "My mechanic was clad in a huge rubber mantle and he wore a sort of hood which fitted tightly around his youthful beardless face and which, as we sped faster and faster into the night, made him look like some pilgrim, or rather, a speed-loving nun. . . . [I]f only the steering-wheel held by the young man who is driving me could always remain the symbol of his talent instead of being the premonition of his death throes." The following summer, both he and the chauffeur spent time together in Versailles, though their leisure activities may have been confined to playing dominoes.

Agostinelli had a common-law wife, Anna Square, and at his request in May 1911 Proust found employment for her as an usher at a theater. The chauffeur apparently wasn't a love interest, however: at the time, that was directed toward Albert Nahmias, a talented young man whom Proust employed as a secretary (which job description did not at that time include typing the manuscript), surrogate gambler and speculator on the stock market, and love object: "If only I were able to change my sex," he wrote Nahmias in November 1911, "alter my age and the way I look, and take on the aspect of a young and beautiful woman so that I could embrace you with all my heart." Instead, he would alter *Albert's* sex, or at least the gender of his name, as a first step toward creating Albertine Simonet.

In May 1913, Agostinelli lost his job and asked Proust to take him on as his personal driver. Since he already had a driver, Proust employed him instead as a secretary-typist, and Agosintelli and Anna moved into the apartment. "It was then that I discovered him," Proust wrote a friend in June 1914, "and that he and his wife became an integral part of my existence." And to another: "I really loved Alfred. It's not enough to say that I loved him; I adored him."

Agnostinelli and Anna evidently had an active sex life, though he was regularly unfaithful to her. What was not uncommon at the time, he may have regarded the providing of some kind of sexual solace to his *patron* to be part of a secretary's job description, though probably not to the extent of intercourse. Proust's sexuality—never high—seems to have been at low ebb by this time.

What grist for jealousy! Proust had to know that his secretary not only "betrayed" him with Anna, but betrayed the both of them with other women—and perhaps other men as well! You can see how a chap might become a dite paranoid in such a situation.

Proust was fabulously generous, routinely tipping waiters twenty francs. Agostinelli accepted whatever was given, and soon was asking for more. Eventually he began to yearn for flight, literally and figuratively, and in December 1913 he left for Monaco (his home) to take flying lessons under the hilariously apt name of "Marcel Swann." To spy on him, and hopefully to bring him back, Proust employed none other than Albert Nahmias, filling the role that in the novel would be performed by Robert de Saint-Loup. In March 1914, Proust ordered an airplane and perhaps a Rolls Royce for Agostinelli, evidently threatening all the while to cancel the orders if the beloved didn't return to Paris.

In the novel, Marcel similarly orders a Rolls and a yacht for Albertine, with the real-life airplane and the fictional yacht each costing the identical sum of 27,000 francs. And the yacht and airplane are each to be engraved with the same stodgy sonnet from Mellarmé:

> A swan of olden times recalls that he
> Splendid yet void of hope to free himself
> Had left unsung the realm of life itself
> When sterility glittered with ennui

Poor, splendid Marcel Swan, isolated in his Paris apartment while the love of his life swanked around the south of France! Then, on April 30, Agostinelli drowned when the plane he was flying crashed into the Mediterranean.

Even as this tumult was happening in his life, Proust was incorporating it (and sometimes even the wording of Agostinelli's letters) into the character of Albertine in *Sodom and Gomorrah*. More than that, he soon began to write the two comparatively short "Albertine" volumes, *The Prisoner* and *The Fugitive*, in which Marcel's obsession ends with Albertine's dying in a fall from a horse.

Of course, few fictional characters are drawn exclusively from one individual. Perhaps Albertine had her real-life female models as well— or perhaps not! It is often true that the least-realized character in a novel is the one who stands for the author. We know ourselves so well (and often so poorly) that we aren't particularly well-equipped to make ourselves come alive on paper. The same can be true of someone else we know very well, in so much complexity that he or she defies our best effort to create a fictional representation. In any event, Albertine doesn't come across (not to me, in any event) with the lovely clarity of the Baron de Charlus or Madame Verdurin, two of the most unforgettable characters in fiction.

Apropos Madame Verdurin: she's one of the great characters in literature, more persuasive to me than Madame Bovary or Anna Karenina, and proof that Proust was able to create female characters as convincing as any of his men. But the *patronne* of course is post-menopausal and no threat to anyone's sexuality.

And *apropos* Charlus: Proust certainly used some of his experiences chasing Alfred when he wrote about the baron's obsession with the pianist (and valet's son) Morel, who at one point begs Charlus for 25,000 francs. And Charlus in turn hires the tailor Jupien to spy on Morel, just as Proust employed his secretary Albert Nahmias. It's as if Proust allocated the tragic elements of that affair to Marcel's romance, and the high comedy to Charlus's.

A reader's comment

"About narrator's 'girl friends' in *La recherche*. Both Alberte, its diminutive Albertine, and Gilberte are highly unusual names for girls in France. . . . On the contrary their masculine forms Albert and Gilbert are quite common.

"Also in the last part of Swann's Way, narrator tells of Gilberte playing at *saute-mouton* [leapfrog]. . . . French boys play it quite often but I when I was a kid I never saw a girl play at it. Also in Proust childhood times girls never wore trousers. Gilberte would have been wearing long robes who would have got caught on her partner when she jumped and sent her crashing head first on the pavement. Now, if Gilberte was in fact Gilbert there is no problem. — Regards, Jean Francois Martinez"

Private Proust

Improbable as it seems, the effete and asthmatic Marcel Proust served a hitch in the French army. He was stationed at Coligny Caserne in the small city of Orléans, south of Paris—and so, I am pleased to say, was I!

Following the Franco-Prussian War that deposed Napoleon III and installed the Third Republic, France imposed conscription on all young men. As an asthmatic and the son of an influential doctor, Marcel could probably have avoided military service, but he chose to volunteer, perhaps to escape from the close confines of his family. Volunteering also enabled him to serve for a year instead of the five imposed upon those who waited for conscription. (His mother suggested that he regard the twelve months as twelve squares of chocolate that he must consume before he was free again.) No doubt he also looked forward to meeting sturdy young men from the lower classes, "whose bodies were more beautiful and agile, their minds more original, their hearts more spontaneous, their characters more natural than in the case of young men I had known before," as he later described them.

Proust went into the army on November 11, 1889, and four days later arrived at Coligny Caserne, on the Faubourg Bannier just a few blocks north of the Orléans train station and city center. He was eighteen. An American draftee would have been hard put to recognize Private Proust's service in the 76th Infantry Regiment. Because of his asthma, he was exempted from morning formations, and indeed he was encouraged to live in private lodgings downtown. (As a matter of fact, I did something similar. Toward the end of my hitch the caserne barracks were renovated and we were moved out to Harbord Barracks, a half-hour bus ride away. Unable to sleep in those crowded quarters, I went AWOL for six months and bunked clandestinely in the office where I worked.) Invited to dine with his captain, and afterward to spend the night, he had to sleep on the bare mattress because he didn't know how to make up his bed.

One-year volunteers like Proust were treated more like officer cadets than common soldiers: to enlist, they were required to have passed their *bac* exams, and to pay for their uniforms and lodging. After the year, they would become non-commissioned officers in the reserve, subject to month-long tours of active duty, and eligible for eventual commissioning as officers. I can, however, find no evidence that Proust actually did any reserve service. (Here too, our military careers were similar.)

In *The Guermantes Way*, Proust describes how the young Marcel arrives in the fictional garrison town of Doncières and takes a cab to the caserne gate, to visit the aristocratic sergeant, Robert de Saint-Loup, who presumably was enlisted for five years: "One of the men on guard went to fetch him, and I waited at the barracks gate, in front of that huge hulk, booming with the November wind, out of which at every moment—for it was six in the evening—men emerged into the street in pairs, staggering unsteadily, as if they were coming ashore in some exotic port where they were temporarily stationed." The moment I read those words, I knew that I was once again arriving at Coligny Caserne, which except for the guard-post looked much as it did in Proust's day. The red-brick buildings were formed in the shape of a *U*, surrounding the parade ground on three sides. These buildings variously served as barracks, mess hall, cafeteria, the post exchange, and offices of the U.S. Army Communications Zone, Europe. Our job, basically, was to send munitions to Germany and in return receive the wounded, if war should break out between NATO and the Warsaw Pact.

In a throwaway line, early in *Sodom and Gormorrah*, Proust mentions passing through the real Orléans by train, which causes him to note that the local cathedral is "quite the ugliest in France."

Today, Coligny Caserne has been taken over by the departmental government for office space (Charles DeGaulle threw the U.S. Army out of France in the 1960s). There's a high school nearby named for the famous writer, and a Rue Marcel Proust not far away. Perhaps they weren't there in 1958, or perhaps I merely overlooked them in the monumental ignorance of the young.

About the Author

Stephen Fall is the pen name of an American journalist and historian who usually writes on topics far moved from early 20th Century French literature. Not to worry! He has been reading Marcel Proust's great novel since it was known in translation as *Remembrance of Things Past*, in the 1920s translation by Charles Scott Moncrieff. When that somewhat musty version was modestly improved in the 1980s by Terence Kilmartin, Stephen acquired that edition as well. Finally, when the "Penguin Proust" was published in the early 2000s, Steve blogged about them online, in words that formed the basis of this little book.

And when that was done, and all the scholarly comment absorbed, Stephen went back and read the 1990s "revision of a revision," in which D. J. Enright brought Kilmartin's version up to date with the most recent French scholarship. His verdict: "Not bad, but I still prefer the Penguin Proust."

Made in the USA
Lexington, KY
26 January 2012